W9-AWO-037

THE SKELETAL SYSTEM

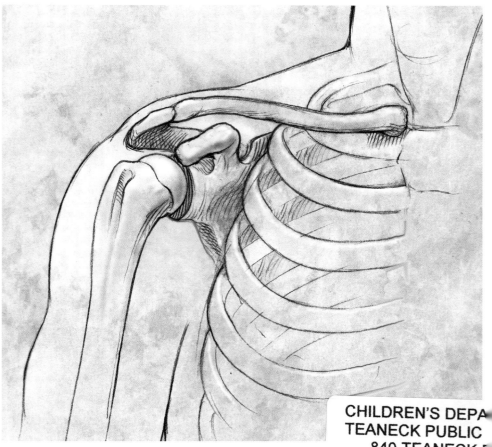

By Susan H. Gray

CHILDREN'S DEPA
TEANECK PUBLIC
840 TEANECK F
TEANECK NJ 0

The Child's World®

Published in the United States of America by the Child's World®
P.O. Box 326, Chanhassen, MN 55317-0326
800-599-READ
www.childsworld.com

Subject adviser:
R. John Solaro, Ph.D.,
Distinguished
University Professor
and Head, Department
of Physiology and
Biophysics, University
of Illinois Chicago,
Chicago, Illinois

Photo Credits: Cover: Artville/Scott Bodell; Corbis: 5, (Michal Heron) 9 (Kevin Schafer), 11 (Susan Solie Patterson), 15 (Jim Cummins), 18; Custom Medical Stock Pictures: 7, 8, 10, 12, 14, 17, 19, 20, 21, 23, 27; PhotoEdit: 16, (Mark Richards), (Tony Freeman), 24 and 25 (Felicia Martinez), 26 (Robert W. Ginn).

The Child's World®: Mary Berendes, Publishing Director

Editorial Directions, Inc.: E. Russell Primm, Editorial Director; Elizabeth K. Martin, Line Editor; Katie Marsico, Assistant Editor; Olivia Nellums, Editorial Assistant; Susan Hindman, Copy Editor; Elizabeth K. Martin, Proofreader; Peter Garnham, Marilyn Mallin, Mary Hoffman, Fact Checkers; Tim Griffin/IndexServ, Indexer; Cian Loughlin O'Day, Photo Researcher; Linda S. Koutris, Photo Selector

Copyright © 2004 by The Child's World®
All rights reserved. No part of this book may be reproduced or utilized in any form or by any means without written permission from the publisher.

Library of Congress Cataloging-in-Publication Data
Gray, Susan Heinrichs.
  The skeletal system / by Susan H. Gray.
     p. cm. — (Living well)
Includes bibliographical references and index.
Contents: What is the skeletal system?—What's inside a bone?—What does the skeleton do?—What holds the skeleton together?—What is cartilage?
  ISBN 1-59296-041-3 (lib. bdg. : alk. paper)
  1. Human skeleton—Juvenile literature. [1. Skeleton. 2. Bones.] I. Title. II. Series: Living well (Child's World (Firm)
  QM101.G695 2004
  612.7'5—dc21   2003006292

TABLE OF CONTENTS

CHAPTER ONE

OUCH!

Clare circled the empty parking lot on her bicycle. This was her new birthday bike, and it was only two days old. Today, she wanted to learn the gears. Clare rode to the far corner of the lot and turned around. Pedaling slowly, she rode along the edge of the pavement. She pressed the little tab to change gears. The bike chain slid smoothly into place. The bike sped up.

Clare thought she would try the next gear. She pushed the little tab again. But just then her front wheel hit a patch of gravel. The bike swung to the left, while Clare went straight forward. She threw out her hands to catch herself. As she fell, her skeleton helped to protect her. Rubbery cushions at the ends of her bones took some of the shock. Her rib cage protected her delicate heart and lungs. Dense

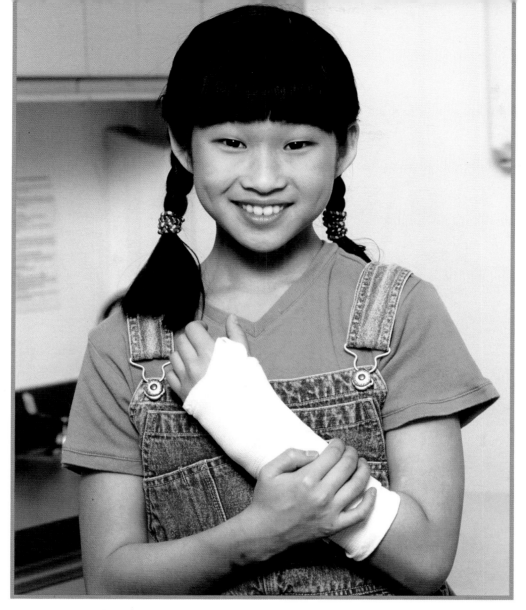

A doctor put a cast on Clare's wrist to help the bones heal correctly.

tissue cords kept her bones from popping out of place. But as she

landed, she felt a sharp pain in her wrist. Clare had broken one of

her bones.

CHAPTER TWO

WHAT IS THE
SKELETAL SYSTEM?

T he bone that Clare broke was one of the 206 bones in her skeletal (SKEL-uh-tul) system. The skeletal system, or skeleton, includes all of the bones in the body.

You can divide the skeleton into two parts. One part is made up of the bones of the axial (AX-ee-ul) skeleton. The other part is made up of bones of the appendicular (AP-pen-DIK-yoo-lur) skeleton. The axial skeleton includes the bones of the head, neck, back, and rib cage. It runs down the middle of the body. The appendicular skeleton includes the bones of the shoulders, arms, hands, hips, legs, and feet. These are the bones that have to do with the **limbs.**

Bones come in all sorts of sizes and shapes. The biggest is the thigh bone. It runs from your hip down to your knee. The tiniest

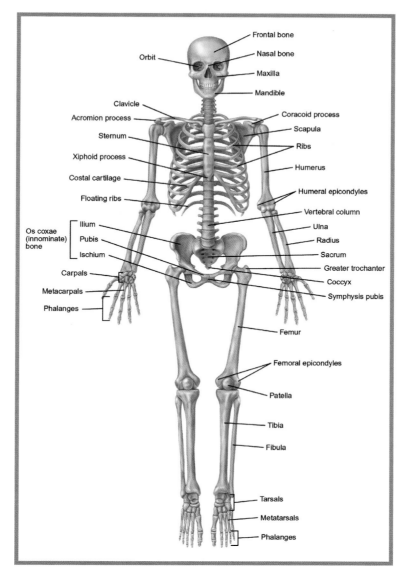

There are 206 bones in the skeletal system,
some very large and some very small.

bone is deep inside your ear. It is called the stirrup, and it is no longer

than a grain of rice.

Bones have four shapes—long, short, flat, and irregular

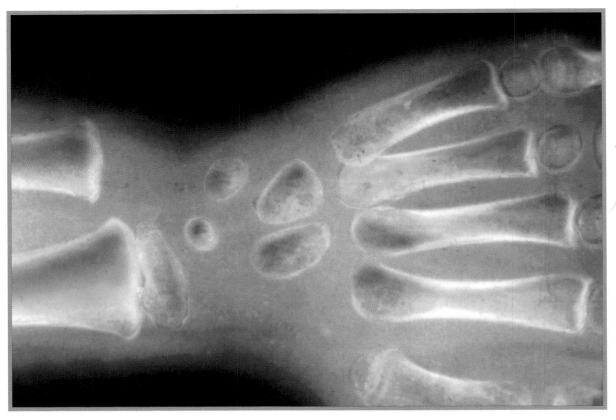

This colorized X ray shows the many short bones that make up the wrist.

(ir-REG-yoo-lur). Long bones are in the arms and legs. They are almost straight and are wide at their ends. Short bones are in the wrists and ankles. They are shaped like little blocks. Flat bones include the ribs, shoulder blades, and some of the skull bones. Irregular bones have all kinds of shapes. Many of these are inside the skull.

CHAPTER THREE

WHAT'S INSIDE A BONE?

The word *skeleton* comes from a Greek word that means

"dried up." But, as we shall see, your skeleton is not dried

up at all. It has parts that are wet and mushy.

On the outside, bones are covered by a tough, thin layer of tissue

full of blood vessels and nerves. The next layer is what we usually

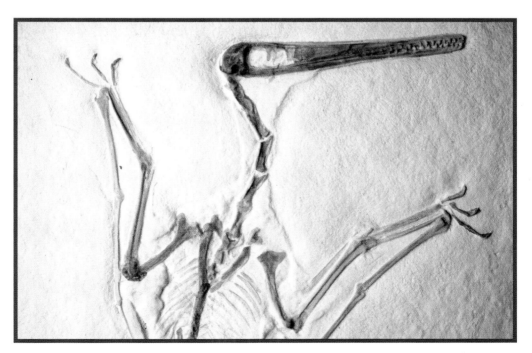

All that is left of this ancient reptile is a fossil of the nonliving parts of its skeleton.

think of as the bone. It is hard and seems to be solid and nonliving. However, it has both living and nonliving parts. The dense, nonliving part is made up of hard minerals. This material is full of tiny holes and tunnels. Living cells rest inside the holes, and blood vessels run through the tunnels. This hard material, with all of its little holes and tunnels, is called compact bone.

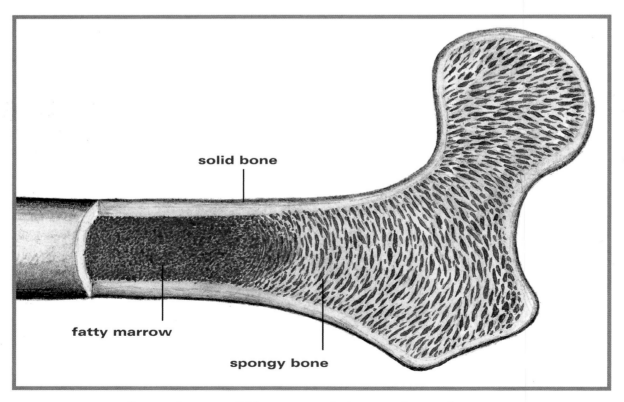

Compact bone, or solid bone, surrounds the spongy bone and marrow.

Deeper inside the dense mate-

rial are bigger holes and

spaces. This is called spongy

(SPUN-jee) bone. It is not

really soft and spongy. It just

looks that way because of all of

the holes.

This baby's bones are full of red marrow, but his older sister's have more yellow marrow.

In the center of a bone is a soft,

pulpy tissue. This is called the marrow (MEHR-roe). Marrow can be

either red or yellow. When a baby is born, its bones are full of red

marrow. The red marrow makes blood cells and platelets. Blood cells

carry food and oxygen to the body's tissues. They also fight infec-

tion. Platelets help blood to clot, or harden, when the body is

injured. As a child grows older, yellow marrow replaces the red mar-

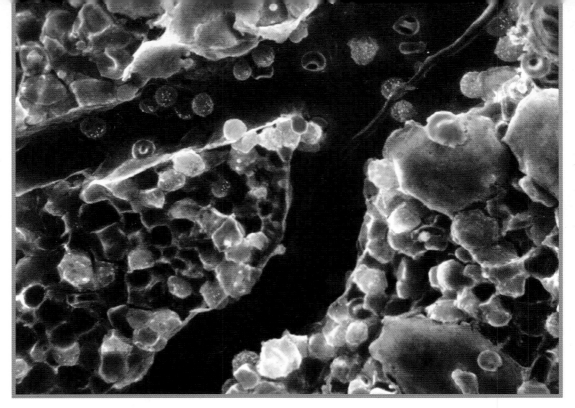

In this scan of yellow bone marrow, you can see large areas of fat cells (shown in yellow).

row in some bones. Yellow marrow is made up mainly of fat cells.

In an adult, only a few bones still have red marrow. These are the

bones of the skull, back, ribs, and hips.

Blood vessels run into and out of bones. They carry food and

oxygen to the cells lying in the little holes. They take **nutrients**

and oxygen to the marrow. They carry away waste materials. And

they bring new blood cells and platelets out to the blood stream.

Skeletons can often tell us plenty about how people lived and died. Scientists who study ancient peoples look at their bones for clues about their lives. For instance, curved leg bones might tell them that someone ate poorly as a child. A thick or very dense place on a bone could be scar tissue. This shows where the bone might have broken and healed. A group of skeletons with strangely shaped neck and shoulder bones could be from people who wore tight bands around their necks.

Scientists have found skulls that are thousands of years old. Some of these skulls have unusual holes in them. Some holes are perfectly square. Some are deep grooves. These holes were made while the people were still alive. Scar tissue formed around the holes, and the people healed. But why would they have these holes at all?

Scientists believe that people did skull surgery thousands of years ago. Back then, no one knew what caused headaches. No one knew about diseases that made people tremble or shake. Doctors at the time might have thought that a hole in the skull would heal them. Maybe a hole would allow the cause of pain to leave. Or maybe an evil spirit would escape through the hole. Today, no one is exactly sure what these holes were for. But this must have been a very popular operation. It was done on men, women, and children. Patients recovered and went on with their lives—maybe even without headaches!

CHAPTER FOUR

WHAT DOES THE SKELETON DO?

The skeleton has a lot of important jobs. For one thing, it helps protect the body's organs. Skull bones protect the brain from injury. The rib cage shields the heart and lungs. Bones in the back protect the spinal cord.

The skeleton also supports the body. It holds you up. If you did not have a skeleton, your body would just be soft and limp.

Your skeleton helps you to move. Muscles are attached to the bones. Together, muscles and bones make your arms and legs move.

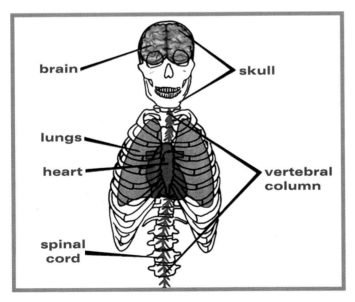

brain
skull
lungs
heart
vertebral column
spinal cord

Some parts of the skeletal system, such as the skull, the vertebral column, and the rib cage, protect important organs in your body.

The skeletal system helps these players move, while also protecting their organs during a tackle.

They work to make your head turn, your jaws chew gum, and your

toes wiggle.

Your bones even do things that you cannot control. They store

materials your body needs. They make blood cells. Bones in your ears

help you to hear!

Calcium is an important material your body needs. Almost

all of the calcium in the body is stored in the skeleton. Just a tiny bit

circulates in the blood. Calcium helps muscles and nerves to work right. It is required for the heart to beat. It also helps blood to clot.

Once in a while, that tiny amount of calcium in the blood gets too

low. Then the body draws calcium from the bones. Calcium moves

out of the skeleton and into the blood. Then the blood level

becomes normal again.

Your skeleton stores the calcium from milk for your body to use when it is needed.

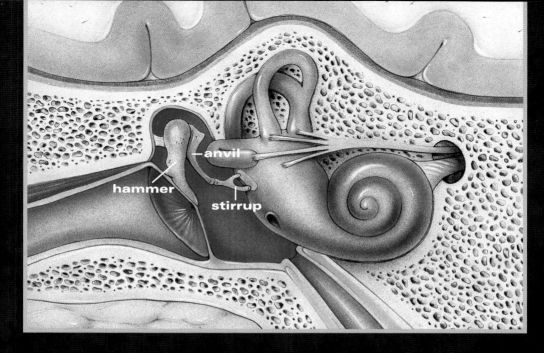

hammer
anvil
stirrup

LITTLE BONES, BIG JOB

The three smallest bones in the body are inside the ear. They are called the hammer, the anvil, and the stirrup. Together, they would not even cover a penny! Although they are tiny, they have a very important job. They work day and night, around the clock. These bones help you to hear.

The bones sit just inside the eardrum. The hammer is shaped like a little club. One end is attached to the eardrum. The other presses against the anvil. The other end of the anvil touches the stirrup.

Every time a sound comes into the ear, these bones go to work. Sounds make the eardrum vibrate back and forth. With each vibration, the little bones move back and forth as well. They send the vibrations deeper into the ear. There, the vibrations are picked up by nerves and cause increased electricity to go to the brain. The brain translates the meaning of each sound. Without these tiniest of bones, we would never hear a thing.

CHAPTER FIVE

WHAT HOLDS THE SKELETON TOGETHER?

A joint is a place where two bones come together. At some joints, the bones can move. Elbows, knees, and ankles are examples of moving joints. At other joints, the bones can't move one bit. The skull has a lot of these joints. There, different bones have grown together over time. Where many of these skull bones meet, the joint is just a wiggly line. It is called a suture (SOO-chur).

At some joints, bones can move just a little. The joints between the ribs and the breastbone are such joints. As you breathe in, these bones move out and up just a little bit.

Joints, such as the elbows and the knees, arm and leg bones move to shoot a basket.

At every joint, some kind of material holds the bones together.

Ligaments (LIG-uh-ments) and tendons (TEN-dunz) have this job.

They keep bones from pulling or slipping apart at the joints.

Ligaments are bands of tough material. They run from one bone

to the next, holding the bones in place. Ligaments are at every joint

that moves. Tendons are also bands of tough material. They connect

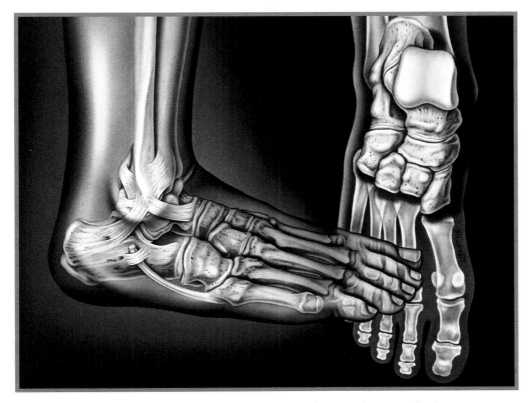

*This drawing shows ligaments connecting the many bones in the foot,
keeping them all in place.*

muscles to bones. Some tendons are easy to find on the body. The biggest, strongest one is the Achilles (uh-KILL-eez) tendon. It is right behind your ankle. It connects the calf muscle to the heel bone.

A few bones do not form joints with other bones. They simply sit alone, within softer tissue. One of these is the hyoid (HI-oid) bone under the chin. Neck and tongue muscles attach to it. Another is the kneecap. It sits inside a tendon.

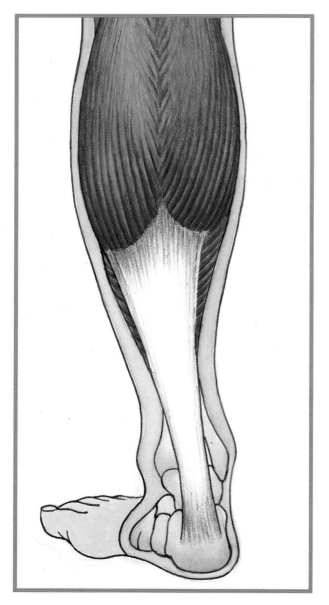

The Achilles tendon, in white, connects the calf muscle to the heel bone. It is the largest tendon in the human body.

CHAPTER SIX

WHAT IS CARTILAGE?

Cartilage (KAR-tuh-lidj) is another tough material found in the skeletal system. Sometimes it is called gristle. Cartilage caps the ends of long bones. A little cartilage cushion lies between each bone in the back. Cartilage also connects the ribs to the breastbone.

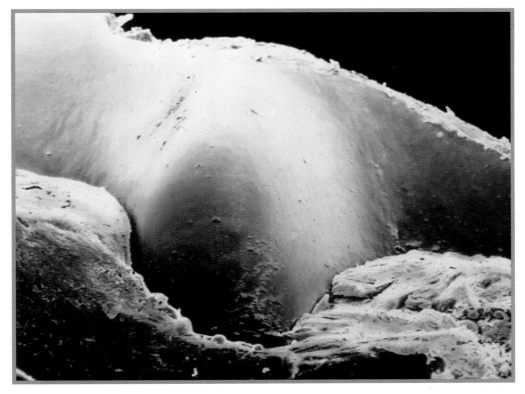

Strong cartilage, or gristle, often grows at the end of bones.

Cartilage is not quite as hard as bone. It can squash and bend a little bit. At the ends of long bones, it makes joints move more smoothly. Cartilage in the knees, for example, makes running and walking smooth and easy.

Cartilage makes running easier and absorbs pressure on your bones as you move.

Cartilage also **absorbs** pressure. The cartilage between the back bones does this. It supports the **spinal column** and cushions it against stress.

Cartilage has one other important job. It forms the models where bones will grow. Long before a baby is born,

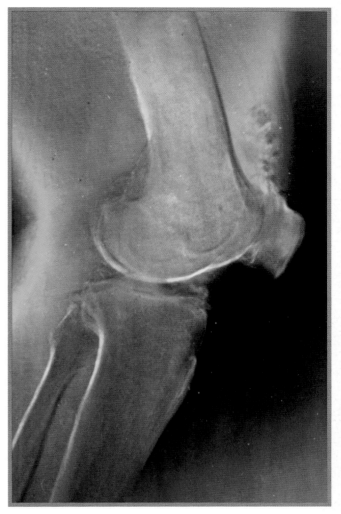

This colorized X ray of an adult's knee shows that there is no cartilage left between the bones. Instead, they rub against each other, causing a painful condition called osteoarthritis.

most of its skeleton is made of car-tilage. Even at birth, parts of many bones are still made of cartilage. Over the years, bones grow and the cartilage slowly disappears. In an adult, most cartilage is found only at the joints.

CHAPTER SEVEN

HEALTHY AND UNHEALTHY SKELETONS

The skeletal system has important work to do. That is why everyone should try to keep it healthy. A healthy skeleton needs plenty of calcium. Milk, cheese, broccoli, and sardines are loaded with calcium. Vitamin D is also important. It helps the body absorb calcium. The best way to get vitamin D is to spend some time in the sun. Be sure to wear sunscreen, however!

Foods high in calcium help keep your skeletal system healthy.

Getting plenty of sun gives bones Vitamin D and helps prevent rickets.
Don't forget the sunscreen!

Sometimes children do not get enough vitamin D. Their grow-

ing bones cannot get the calcium they need. These children get a

disease called rickets (RIK-uts). Their bones are weak and soft

Not getting enough calcium in your diet can cause osteoporosis when you are older.

instead of strong and hard. The skeleton does not grow as tall as it

should. The leg bones become curved.

Sometimes adults do not get enough calcium to their bones.

They get a disease called osteoporosis (OSS-tee-oh-pore-OH-siss).

The dense bone material becomes thin. Little holes appear in it. The bones become delicate and break easily.

The skeleton is truly amazing. It takes care of the body in many ways. So we should always take care of it.

Take good care of your skeletal system—it lets you do the things you love!

CHILDREN'S DEPARTMENT
TEANECK PUBLIC LIBRARY
TEANECK, NEW JERSEY 07666

Glossary

absorb (ab-ZORB) To absorb something is to soak it up.

ancient (AYN-shunt) A thing or people that are ancient are very, very old.

calcium (KAL-see-uhm) Calcium is an important material the body needs for healthy bones and teeth.

eardrum (IHR-druhm) The eardrum is a thin piece of tissue in the ear that picks up sound waves.

limbs (LIMZ) Limbs are the arms and legs.

nutrients (NOO-tree-uhnts) Nutrients are the things found in foods that are needed for life and health.

spinal column (SPYE-nuhl KOHL-uhm) The spinal column is the series of bones running down the back.

vibrate (VYE-brate) To vibrate means to move back and forth very quickly.

Questions and Answers about the Skeletal System

Which bone is the longest? Your thigh bone, the femur, is the longest bone in your body. It is about one fourth of your total height!

What is the funny bone? The funny bone isn't really a bone at all! It's a nerve that runs near a bone called the humerus. So when you hit your elbow, it isn't really a bone that is hurting, it's a nerve.

What happens when I crack my knuckles? When you crack your knuckles, you are really pulling apart the bones held together by the joints in your fingers. This creates a bubble in the fluid between the bones. The bubble quickly pops, and the fluid returns, making that annoying noise!

I broke my arm. How does a cast help my arm heal? The doctor put a cast on your arm so that the bones would stay in the right places to grow back together. The broken bones will grow new cells and blood vessels to cover up the broken ends of the bone and close them up. By the time your cast comes off, your arm will be almost as good as new!

Did You Know?

- On some bones, you can easily see a hole where a blood vessel passes through. The next time you eat chicken, look closely at the leg bones. You will see tiny holes that lead right to the marrow.

- Babies are born with more than 270 bones. As they grow, some of these bones fuse together.

- An accident or disease can cause the body to get low on blood cells. Then, red marrow replaces yellow marrow in the bones. The new red marrow makes blood cells until the body is back to normal.

- Tiny bones called sesamoid (SESS-uh-moid) bones rest all alone inside some tendons. They are not connected to other bones. They are called sesamoid because some look like sesame seeds.

- Humans have seven neck bones. Giraffes also have seven bones in the neck.

How to Learn More about the Skeletal System

At the Library

Silverstein, Alvin, Virginia Silverstein, and Robert Silverstein.
The Skeletal System.
New York: Twenty-First Century Books, 1994.

Simon, Seymour.
Bones: Our Skeletal System.
New York: Morrow Junior, 1998.

Taylor, Barbara.
Skeleton.
New York: DK Publishing, 1998.

On the Web

Visit our home page for lots of links about the skeletal system:
http://www.childsworld.com/links.html
Note to Parents, Teachers, and Librarians: We routinely verify our
Web links to make sure they're safe, active sites—so encourage
your readers to check them out!

Through the Mail or by Phone

ARTHRITIS FOUNDATION
P.O. Box 7669
Atlanta, GA 30357-0669
800-283-7800
http://www.arthritis.org

NATIONAL OSTEOPOROSIS FOUNDATION
1232 22nd Street, N.W.
Washington, D.C. 20037-1292
202-223-2226
http://www.nof.org

NATIONAL INSTITUTE OF ARTHRITIS AND
MUSCULOSKELETAL AND SKIN DISEASES
Information Clearinghouse
National Institutes of Health
1 AMS Circle
Bethesda, Maryland 20892-3675
301-495-4484
http://www.niams.nih.gov

Index

About the Author

Susan H. Gray has a bachelor's and a master's degree in zoology, and has taught college-level anatomy and physiology courses. In her 25 years as an author, she has written many medical articles, grant proposals, and children's books. Ms. Gray enjoys gardening, traveling, and playing the piano and organ. She has traveled twice to the Russian Far East to give organ workshops to church musicians. She also works extensively with American and Russian friends to develop medical and social service programs for Vladivostok, Russia. Ms. Gray and her husband, Michael, live in Cabot, Arkansas.